volume 112 of the yale series of younger poets

Yale UNIVERSITY PRESS | NEW HAVEN AND LONDON

# we play

## a

# game

**DUY DOAN**

FOREWORD BY CARL PHILLIPS

Published with assistance from a grant to honor James Merrill.

Yale University Press books may be purchased in quantity for educational,
business, or promotional use. For information, please e-mail sales.press@yale
.edu (U.S. office) or sales@yaleup.co.uk (U.K. office).

Designed by Nancy Ovedovitz and set in The Sans type by Integrated Publishing
Solutions. Printed in the United States of America.

Library of Congress Control Number: 2017955730
ISBN 978-0-300-23088-8 (hardcover : alk. paper)
ISBN 978-0-300-23087-1 (paperback : alk. paper)

A catalogue record for this book is available from the British Library.

This paper meets the requirements of ANSI/NISO Z39.48-1992
(Permanence of Paper).

10 9 8 7 6 5 4 3 2

*For Jane Marie Yorke*

I learned to catch the trout's moon whisper; I

Drifted how many hours I never knew

—*Hart Crane*

# contents

## Tìm

## Mà

## foreword

The title of Duy Doan's book—*We Play a Game*—is deceptively straightforward. Indeed, there are references to games everywhere in these poems: from games of sport, like soccer and boxing, to prosodic games like the formal one that the pantoum can be, to the tongue twisters of "Three Tongue Twisters":

> *Bốn bạn bán bốn bàn bẩn.*
> Four friends sell four dirty tables.

i. Personal ad

> *Con chim tim tím tìm*
> *con chó trẻ trẻ.*
> *Con chó trẻ trẻ chê*
> *con chim tim tím.*

Purple-hearted bird
seeks
youngish dog.

Youngish dog is
not impressed by

purple-hearted bird.

ii. Dessert

*Cô con cần cắt trái cây.*
*Trái cây cần cắt con cây.*

Auntie has to slice up the fruit.

The fruit had better hide the children
of the tree.

iii. Breakup

*Bồ Bố bỏ Bố hôm qua.*
*Hôm qua bồ Bố hôn con,*
*hôn con hôn con hôn con hôn con.*

Daddy's girlfriend left him yesterday.

Yesterday
daddy's girlfriend kissed me,
kissed me kissed me kissed me kissed me.

Clearly there's no narrative to this poem, though I can track a
progression from we-can't-always-get-what-we-want in "Personal
ad" to the vulnerability of children in "Dessert" to the father who
loses what he wants—possibly to his own child—in "Breakup." The
poem doesn't strike me as especially lyric, either. The poem risks
seeming an exercise, a "mere" game. For me, though, what emerges
from that risk is an invitation—not so much to consider these
particular three tongue twisters, but to consider first the tongue
twister itself, as a form—what is it?—and then to consider its
effects. A tongue twister is a grouping of words that are difficult to
say both distinctly and quickly when strung together. In English, the
difficulty is usually the result of alliteration—a pileup of consonants.

In Doan's poem, we can see that alliteration also characterizes a tongue twister in Vietnamese, but the diacritical marks above various vowels suggest another difficulty at two levels—vowel and intonation. The same word means something different, depending on the mark above it, as the twister of the poem's epigraph makes immediately clear. Or as Doan states outright in another poem, "History Lesson from Anh Hai":

Bà Nội used to always tell me, *Đi tu đi con*. But I know
The difference between *tu* and *tù* is one mark.

The one mark turns the word for "novitiate" or "seminary/convent" to the word for "prison," Doan points out in his notes to the poem.

So much for the definition. As to a tongue twister's effects, I'd say there are two: in an effort to say the words of a twister, we are thwarted by the words themselves from saying what we want to say; and as we find ourselves tripped up by the actual words, we also end up saying what we didn't intend. What to do when language is a primary means of communication, and yet language has the power to at once confound and betray our best efforts to say a thing? Ultimately this is the question on which "Three Tongue Twisters" invites me to meditate.

A quieter, not at all unrelated, and no less important question of the poem, thanks to its juxtaposing of Vietnamese and English, is: What does it mean to live in two languages or, maybe more exactly, in that emptier space (the white space of the page) between? Wisely, Doan never answers this question directly, but the poems themselves suggest that to work with and within language, if a game, is a game as complicated and delicate as soccer—an obvious enthusiasm of Doan's—where to "narrate the passes" is one thing, to initiate and complete the passes is another thing entirely:

First the irretrievable, then
Iniesta's stroke to release Messi
gleaming into the English Channel:

Was it pragmatism or panache.
Is it something you can kill.
["Dancing School"]

It took me awhile to understand why soccer is so frequently referred
to in *We Play a Game,* but I now think Doan thinks of soccer as, in
a sense, the prime model for how excellence can be attained not
through individual but through *collective* talent aimed at a common
goal. It's as if soccer is its own Olympus, with stars like Messi and
Iniesta as its gods. Which is to say, soccer becomes an ideal that the
rest of life gets measured against. And in the taking of that measure,
Doan tells us that everything else is found wanting.

One important manifestation, in these poems, of a failure to
work collectively toward a common good is that of family. As Tolstoy
famously said, "Every unhappy family is unhappy in its own way," and
the particular way for the family in Doan's poems has in part to do
with generational estrangement from cultural origins. Doan is second-
generation Vietnamese-American, and the poems often reckon with
the conundrum of having been born and grown up in the United States
while having parents who were born in Vietnam and still have family
there. The conundrum's apparent right away at the level of language:

When my brother
and sisters and I talk about Vietnamese
pronouns,

we're ghosts
reminiscing about facial expressions

and what it was like to have teeth and skin.
["First-Person Plural"]

It's telling, that in the course of this poem the first-person "we"
routinely gets lost in favor of "you," "I," "he," and "she." Language

itself—along with the culture attached to it—estranges the children from their parents. How to work together, if language—tricky game, again—actually hinders communication?

So that's one unhappiness. Another is more hidden but referred to directly in a few places: a mother strikes her daughter to the ground ("Crayola"), a father uses a keychain "with 30 keys, maybe more" to hit his son in the head ("Wristwatch"); there's mention of a bullet that may or may not be metaphorical:

The bullet
tears
but we don't say
it has hands.

One night I look up
and bang
our family
has torn our family
apart forever.
["Post-mortem with My Little Brother"]

Though not an excuse, it seems worth mentioning that these violent parents, in coming to the United States, came fresh from a space of violence larger than themselves, a space of war and its attendant atrocities:

Bà Nội cried the night dad disappeared into a jungle.
It was a sad time. A nun and monk were made to fornicate in the
     street.
Once I heard about a monk who died setting himself on fire.
["History Lesson from Anh Hai"]

Who can say the degree to which violence gets passed on, as history, but also maybe as a kind of genealogy?

Deliberately, I believe, Doan does not push at this subject of family violence. In many ways *We Play a Game* is its own nimble game of avoidance, wherein the refusal to stay with any troubling subject for too long enables the book to operate as a photographic negative: what isn't there implies what is. Another way, though, to think of the book is as the verbal enactment of a self refusing to be narrowly defined—in the name of, variously, freedom and sometimes sheer sanity. Also in the name, perhaps, of something as simple as honesty. We are more than our race alone, Doan suggests, as we are also more than, in isolation, our family history, our gender, our sexuality, or what sports we follow. Humans are complicated, multifarious—and the arrangement of the poems here reinforces that: poems of tenderness and intimacy occur between poems of family violence; one moment we're in Vietnam, and the next in a suburban front yard in the United States; the soccer greats find their analogs in the many animals—cats, especially—that populate these poems. What holds everything together is Doan's particular sensibility, of course, which, if pressed, I'd sum up as restlessness as the one tool left for survival. If you never stop moving, and if you keep exchanging one costume, as it were, for another, it's pretty hard to get caught. No leaning heavily on the confessional mode, then, for this poet; no leaning solely on identity, or on one piece of it in particular. This might look like an inability to commit, but I see it as an example of the skillful restraint that characterizes Doan's poems. The short poem "You" is a good instance:

You never told her about Jesus. The way
the truth plants itself in good soil
only to come forth later into the sun
is like the path to salvation. The serpent told you
to take her—you made love near the sheep's gate
where small stones, like ticks, burrowed
into her backside, and you asked about her husband.
It was nearly dawn when she returned to him.

For a while, you whistled to yourself.
The ears of a ewe nearby twitched once,
then once again, its two eyes
lit sharply against its black face.

The title alone withholds identity. We don't know the gender of this
you, let alone race or profession. The you is associated with Chris-
tianity, but also with one of Christianity's taboos, adultery. Doan
casts no judgment one way or the other on this subject. Instead,
via juxtaposition—not resolution—we're shown a sheep whose
ears move, and whose eyes may or may not have witnessed the
adultery. But what is adultery, to a sheep? What is adultery, in
terms of right or wrong, when removed from the moral construct
of Christianity? Somewhere in here, Doan leaves us room to con-
template these questions and, by extension, the larger question
of morality itself, a product of the self-consciousness that makes
us human, distinguishes us from sheep—but who is happier, the
human or the sheep? What is happiness, though, without the
ability to know happiness *as* happiness? What is guilt, versus what
is guilt *for?* This is poem as invitation, not as argument, not as
declaration.

   *We Play a Game* includes two long poems, and while they don't
exactly frame the book, they are the anchoring poems of the book's
first and last sections. Considered together, they convince me that
the governing theme of this book is the impulse toward transforma-
tion (as opposed to the actual attainment of transformation). As the
speaker of Jarrell's "The Woman at the Washington Zoo" says, "You
know what I was,/You see what I am: change me, change me!" The
first of Doan's long poems, "Love Trinkets," presents itself as a
catalogue of past lovers, each attached to a memorial anecdote.
Here's the opening section:

One lover was bored and kissed me once
while sitting on her father's kimono.

-

One lover kissed me with his mother's
bridal robe within sight.


-

One lover was bold and touched
me once behind a door, but it was her cousin
Vandie, the one who never looked at me, that I loved.


-

One lover was kind, so kind, in kissing
me at all.

In the course of the poem, we learn that this speaker has had many
lovers, same-sex and not, sometimes monogamously, other times
polyamorously, in childhood and as an adult. Here is the constant
shifting from one thing to another that I mentioned earlier. But
there's a picaresque quality to this poem: the rogue hero, the epi-
sodic nature that requires changes in locale and circumstance,
though the hero himself cannot change. For me, the tension of
the picaresque lies in how the forward movement from episode
to episode, suggesting change/development/possibility, rubs up
against the hero's refusal and/or inability to admit that he himself
cannot fundamentally change. And in that tension is the bittersweet
sorrow that runs through so much of Doan's work—bittersweet,
because not without surges of joy, good intention—which is to
say, hope.

Implied in "Love Trinkets" is that somewhere in the communion
between at least two people toward a shared goal (back to soccer),
there might be a chance for something better than the life we're
living. Or at least the hope of this is implied. This comes up again,
differently, in Doan's other long poem, "The Roundworm Travels
Up from the Foot." Rather than changing episodically from section

to section, this poem instead rings the changes on a handful of activities that keep getting returned to, most notably dancing, boxing, and—twice—a mermaid birth. The poem opens with this sentence: "Survival instincts: I turn myself into a smaller target." And not much later we're told that this is what's required in boxing: "To make yourself into a smaller target." To be a smaller target in boxing is to be harder to hit. In a crowd of dancers, it is to become anonymous, to not stand out so much as a target:

> In the dark, with the music, there's no need to be a silhouette; your shoulders can be square to others. One goal: to be a string undulating between two fixed points.

A classic position, of course, for turning oneself into a smaller target is to assume the fetal position. This brings me to the mermaid birth, the term for when the fetus emerges completely enclosed in the amniotic sac—is technically not born yet:

> The amniotic sac is intact and someone has to puncture it. Then baby's song: so brave and so beautiful. His rotator cuff, the examining table, unused forceps and ventouse.

> Silver nitrate
> eye drops: then Judy Garland is in color.

The last lines refer to the old practice of putting silver nitrate in the baby's eyes at birth as a stay against infection. Doan suggests that this is the moment when the baby sees in color, experiencing that moment in *The Wizard of Oz* when the world shifts from black and white to color—that's the obvious transformation, but of course the world has itself been entirely transformed in that moment for Dorothy, the character played in the movie by Judy Garland.

The second reference to a mermaid birth closes the poem:

The amniotic sac is intact and someone has to puncture it. Then
mother's wooing: so overwhelming, so alluring. New Order,
Erasure, Lorde, glitter, eyeliner. Judy Garland is in color.

Here, birth is conflated with dancing at a club—or at least with
things associated with a club, the music that might be played there,
the drag and camp that come to mind with the bringing together
of glitter, eyeliner, and Judy Garland, and there's been an earlier
reference to Ecstasy, a common enough club drug, drug of
transformation:

Ecstasy turns us into moths.

I'm an embryo in the mother's womb.

Doan seems to suggest that maybe both things are possible—
or we have to believe they are—namely, to disappear in the
crowd and thereby become a smaller target, no longer standing
out as a complicated human being with a torn history; and to be
born into otherness, transformed by music, drugs, makeup, and
transported to a world that leaves this comparatively colorless
one behind.

Doan's book could have ended here, but I think it's right that it
doesn't. I think it's honest, that it doesn't. Doan returns instead to
earlier themes—animals and their dexterity, failure in love, family as
lonely company, the sexual ambiguity of a rickshaw boy who seems
to have seduced his ride or at least considered it; and soccer. But this
time, soccer as an art form that is as vulnerable to corruption—by
association—as the kind of art that has historically been looted, has
had to survive "the underworld/where it was used as currency."
Messi's triumphs are a part of history; but history also includes
"the fire outside the opera house in Berlin"—the 1933 event, Nazi-

promoted, at which Hitler's associate, Goebbels, spoke. These two events do not rhyme, Doan insists—yet, in history at least, they coexist. Triumph and atrocity. Even as the self, Doan's poems suggest, amounts to the coexistence of many parts, not all of them attractive, each one an aspect of identity, most parts more unresolvable than we'd like to admit. Doan's poems remind me of this by enacting it— that's their restless gift.

*Carl Phillips*

we play a game

*Ca*

## we play a game using tomatoes

*cà*
Whoever steps on the seeds

*ca*
loves to sing on penis,

*chua*
and will patiently endure his

*chua*
future wife's nagging.

*cá*
The fish in the pond feed looking up.

*cá*
They play on our expectations

*chùa*
and hopes of pleasing others

*chùa*
and hopes of pleasing ourselves.

*ca*
We've never gone that far,

*ca*
we've never been with each other.

*cà*
We want to eat each other,

*chua*
eat each other whole.

## from the provinces

It was a large no-bedroom house.
All week it rained
three, four hours at a time, stopped for one,
then started up again,

washing away repeatedly sandal
prints and tire marks
from the clay-orange tiles running
the entire length of the driveway,

and leaving the wooden handrails
of the ghost bridge
soft enough to carve names in cursive
with your fingernail.

Every night we sat on something hard.
I brought a bottle of tequila
with a worm in it. People
said there was dancing.

None of the girls knew how to cook.
I ruined one of the pots—
burned it dry,
scarred it with a serving spoon.

One night while it was clear out,
two ducks made for the water
and quacked at each humungous grapefruit
in the trees along the way:

Iris, Violet, Mayflower, Rainwater.
A half-tailed cat stalked them on the way.
The rain started again.
Every cigarette was lit with great care.

## romanticizing vietnam

Praise whoever shook grief's rattle.
There, where they have no winter,

they sing about the moon's pallor crescent,
and hear it reflected on the pond.

A lotus stem to stir the silt,
they make rhyme fall on neutral tones.

In the pink light, I'm drunk
with the moon, chock-full of poems

to a dead brother. I sing into a paper lantern.
Its panes rattle, framing

against the wall my slow
dance. I fail to see

meaning in the white lotus
blossoming in the swamp.

# love trinkets

*After Marie Howe*

**1.**

One lover was bored and kissed me once
while sitting on her father's kimono.

-

One lover kissed me with his mother's
bridal robe within sight.

-

One lover was bold and touched
me once behind a door, but it was her cousin
Vandie, the one who never looked at me, that I loved.

-

One lover was kind, so kind, in kissing
me at all.

-

**2.**

Orange-lime sorbet, my first love loved me innocently.
Her father gave her a big-wheel shaped fan
that she never used but which I admired

even though it opened in a clumsy way.
You had to snap it open with pace while dipping it.
You had to force the ink down the way you do with a Victorian pen—
something like that.

-

One crush and I were one-minute friends.
We watched the clock together on April 16th.

-

One lover played the trumpet, but I
played the trombone which has so much more real estate to it.

-

When we first met, my partner and I scheduled
regular meetings to look at one another.

The earth shook, a portal opened, we stepped through it.

-

One love and I kissed
under the Tree of Enlightenment
and renamed our children Eva and Eve.
Both girls sit at the right hand of their mother.

The same love and I
fell asleep under that same tree
but forgot to wonder about the strangeness of
*having to have a body*
and so lost our humanity
but then remembered
to regain it.

-

One crush and I shared orange slices after
soccer games.
Parents packed sliced oranges with the rind still on
in ziplock bags and kept
them in coolers.

The same crush let me touch him for a long time. The next day I
    ignored him
until there were other people around
and then I cracked a joke at his expense. But that was normal
    behavior
because we were always breaking each other's balls like that.



-

3.
Engagement Ring

You said it was a starling once.
The gold in the bird's feathers
got left behind.
The wind plays tax collector, the mountain
alchemist. The starling, black all over.

Your family gave my family a dowry.
I kept the bills folded, clipped together
in a pillowcase close to my ear.

The path the black bird takes
we will travel, until we arrive
at a screened porch. Arboretum
within walking distance.
You promised me.

\-

## 4.
Proposal
(Lines adapted from Wong Kar Wai's *Days of Being Wild*)

How long have we known each other.

>A long time.
>I've forgotten.

My cousin's getting married soon.

>Really? Give her my best wishes.

She said
she'll be moving in with her husband's family.


>Right.

I have to find someplace else to live.

I'd like to live with you.


>Sure.


How will I tell my dad.

>Tell him what.

About us.

>What about us?

-

5.
Polyamorous

I'm the rabbit
eating flowers off
the lawn.

You stop to admire me
on your run. I regard
you with my prey eye. I never

stop chewing.
It's not an act of predation—
I know this, you think,

not because
I understand
your intentions,

but because I can elude you—
you're far enough away. We have
this understanding.

In love
I am the weaker one
because you have no need

to possess me—
the boy with the rabbit's diet.
You stop to admire

me on your run. You stop
for another. Little
patches

of weeds and their flowers become
an endless
string of introductions.


-

6.
My new love and I met the other day;
she said to meet her near the water
where we saw the moon that one time:
so corny and so cheesy,
but I love it when she's
like that. We learned to
catch the trout's moon whisper.


-

7.
*Beautiful, wonderful, amazing, fantastic:* three-syllable hyperbole
    when playing the coquette.
*Lovely, little,* lastly *likely:* two-syllable hyperbole when listing
    features to describe the coquette.


-

8.
One crush was an INFP. She said the 46th thing
she ever learned
was that all extroverts and all flirtatious men look like idiots.

\-

**9.**
My boyhood love and I squirreled away each other's bodies.
"Let's play lady."
In a giant cardboard box of country western clothing
we flashed fans at one another:
Who could be more garish,
who could be more coquettish?


\-

**10.**
One love enchanted me with her cleverness
and so I loved her the most.
I tried to take a selfie of us once but goofed the whole thing.

"Hold the river closer, Narcissus,"
she told me. "Hold the river closer."

**arrangements**


hail changes the shape of a city.
the sun, shy above the

sound of shattering.
no beast was ever as wild

as the dimpling of a pond
cooled by hailstones.

out of various glass bottles,
one rhythm approaches

monotony, when it is hardest
to trace what is random.

the illusion of synchronicity:
the gazelle the cheetah.

## dancing school

> Four deer practiced leaping over your fences.
> —Elizabeth Bishop

1. Find the radius
   of Xavi's positive
   Influence Aura.


2. Puyol on the corner:

   Describe the body's shape. Is it favorable
   or inauspicious.


3. First the irretrievable, then
   Iniesta's stroke to release Messi
   gleaming into the English Channel:

   Was it pragmatism or panache.
   Is it something you can kill.


4. Xavi, Messi and Iniesta and two defenders, all in a canoe.
   Iniesta alone in the canoe.

   Narrate the passes.

## duet

> Night time is the right time . . .
> —Ray Charles and Margie Hendricks

She had me in the car. I came forward like a song.
We did it before temple, after temple, between prayers.
The windows echoed her mantras, our cries warmed the air.
Two peaks merged, then sank below the clouds.

We did it before temple, after temple, between prayers.
Her stomach began to show and people asked us not to come.
Two peaks merged, then sank below the clouds.
Night and day, everything was changing.

. . . . .

Her stomach began to show and people asked her not to come.
My mother was all alone when I was born.
*Night and day.* Everything was changing.
The radio started playing rhythm and blues.

My mother was all alone when I was born—
The windows echoed her mantras, our cries warmed the air,
The radio started playing rhythm and blues.
She had me In a car. I came forward like a song.

## spelling out my name, or proof of the military industrial complex


delta uniform yankee
bravo alfa
delta oscar alfa november

## first-person plural


When my brother
and sisters and I talk about Vietnamese
pronouns,

we're ghosts
reminiscing about facial expressions

and what it was like to have teeth and skin.
Is it the lock's
rattling home we
miss? The bald
spoon soundlessly departing the mouth?

*Em—*
I had a younger
brother, I had dominion over him. *Em—*
I had a younger sister,
I hardly ever looked at her.

Getting hit
never made us
any closer.

*Chị*, you're the oldest, you get
hit first.

You were scared you'd lose your hearing,

then your hair;

gaining too much weight, and then losing too much.

*Thím* who won and lost a lot at cards, *Chú* who
tried to stop her. *Mấy em* who may
or may not have sensed loss

through talk about the weather, people

at their parents' work.

*Mẹ* told me about
each of *Thím*'s
relapses over the phone; she could make
it one week before telling any of us. *Bố*
neither confirmed nor denied any of this.

*Ông Nội* existed in a celestial
manor; untouched,
starch-calloused collar,
punctual cough.
He knew. Or,
he didn't.

*Bác* who is wise, who has more wisdom
than our parents.

*Cô*
gave me a foreign coin once. I don't remember
the denomination.

We trade pronouns like currency.
52 Pickup until there are no betas left.

*Út* who picked up the cards until we got too
old for that game,

or up until the last time we were
all in a car together. *Anh, chị, em,*

*mình—*
Some birds mistook
us for food humans once. None of us knew
what to call them.

## ask mr. owl

*How many licks does it take ...*

How many times can
I be forgiven?

*Seventy-seven times
seven times.*

How many
baptisms do we get?

*Seventy-seven
times seven.*

*Seventy-seven times
seven baptisms. We get*

*seventy-seven
times seven baptisms.*

## spelling out my name in vietnamese, or proof of the military industrial complex


delta oscar alfa november
bravo alfa
delta uniform yankee

## mother's dirge

Because our family is from the countryside,
Your father liked falling from high places.
Limber feet make expert tree climbers.
The coconut—meat for eating, fiber for the buttonmaker.

Your father liked falling from high places.
Upon landing, he smiles. I carry my share.
The coconut—meat for eating, fiber for the buttonmaker.
Where the bend in the trunk begins matters most.

Upon landing, he smiles. I carry my share.
Husband and wife walk home, avoiding rice paddies.
Where the bend in the trunk begins matters most.
Even if they are full, trees that stand straight: avoid climbing.

Husband and wife walk home, avoiding rice paddies.
Your grandmother warned me many times over.
Even if they are full, trees that stand straight: avoid climbing.
But we were young, the city called to us like a wilderness.

Your grandmother warned me many times over.
Saigon is big, too busy, lacking decency.
But we were young, the city called to us like a wilderness.
The day he died, the sun heated the cement too hot for bare feet.

Saigon is big, too busy, lacking decency.
Afterwards, home brought no comfort.
The day he died, the sun heated the cement too hot for bare feet.
The New World Hotel stands fourteen stories.

Afterwards, home brought no comfort,
Because tragedy cannot save face.
The New World Hotel stands fourteen stories.
Everyone here must remember my new dress last fall,

Because tragedy cannot save face.
Our neighbors recount our tale with great skill and detail.
Everyone here must remember my new dress last fall.
With the white of his palms alone, your father made us a living.

Our neighbors recount our tale with great skill and detail.
The palm trees out front aren't tall enough.
With the white of his palms alone, your father made us a living.
Even when we were promised, I could see he had ability.

The palm trees out front aren't tall enough.
Mind your father, improve yourself, head upwards.
Even when we were promised, I could see he had ability.
He climbed until he got us to the city.

Mind your father, improve yourself, head upwards.
Limber feet make expert tree climbers.
Because our family is from the countryside,
He climbed until he got us to the city.

**y o u**


You never told her about Jesus. The way
the truth plants itself in good soil
only to come forth later into the sun
is like the path to salvation. The serpent told you
to take her—you made love near the sheep's gate
where small stones, like ticks, burrowed
into her backside, and you asked about her husband.
It was nearly dawn when she returned to him.
For a while, you whistled to yourself.
The ears of a ewe nearby twitched once,
then once again, its two eyes
lit sharply against its black face.

*Tim*

# three tongue twisters

*Bốn bạn bán bốn bàn bẩn.*
Four friends sell four dirty tables.

**i.** Personal ad

*Con chim tim tím tìm*
*con chó trẻ trẻ.*
*Con chó trẻ trẻ chê*
*con chim tim tím.*

Purple-hearted bird
seeks
youngish dog.

Youngish dog is
not impressed by

purple-hearted bird.

**ii.** Dessert

*Cô con căn cắt trái cây.*
*Trái cây căn cắt con cây.*

Auntie has to slice up the fruit.

The fruit had better hide the children
of the tree.


iii. Breakup

    *Bõ Bố bỏ Bố hôm qua.*
    *Hôm qua bõ Bố hôn con,*
    *hôn con hôn con hôn con hôn con.*

Daddy's girlfriend left him yesterday.

Yesterday
daddy's girlfriend kissed me,
kissed me kissed me kissed me kissed me.

## bridge ghosts

*Ma (ghost)*

Truth was furthest from a lie we ever got in the lifetime.


*Má (mom)*

Every bridge in this province runs East and West.

The spirits in these firecrackers
have no ancestors here anymore.


*Mà (although, but)*

Smoke is only a symbol.
Try to reunite them. Start by finding a mother.
Here comes one who sweeps
the paper and the ash.

## crayola

We had a statue of Mary on our lawn on a pedestal overlooking
the monkey grass. We played at her feet

the lawn a stern town square. My father the tax collector

part of his route scaly apartment buildings near a homeless bridge
found shards Mary's face a case of empty beer bottles

everything covered in piss some of it soaking through the cardboard
   box he
used to carry her home to our mother

who cleaned each shard in the sink like she was washing
dinner knives. They said a rosary together.

Like Jesus Mary was resurrected after a few days. My mother
the craftswoman who for some change made Christmas
   centerpieces

out of felt reindeer and twigs carrying red berries made out of foam

set Mary on the mantelpiece where she stayed
until I was about eight when my grandfather came to visit

and took Mary and set her on a pedestal he'd placed on the lawn

draped in a blue green cloak
the fringe fat with glitter substantial as geese

our neighbor Uncle Jim who mowed our lawn whenever he mowed
   his own

watching the whole time.

The cloak turned cerulean with a little rain. One of my sisters
watering the lawn once clumsy put the sprinkler

too near the pedestal and the spouting water found its way
just beyond the glitter of Mary's fringes and lit up bits of sky

before an abrupt cupping sound the height of my sister's head

which was the sound of my mother's palm creating suction
out of my sister's ear

and she sort of half knelt on top of a mound of monkey grass

and then half fell over. My mother standing over her
half expecting her to cry or get up.

After a few minutes I was able to resurrect her.

## poem with a rat in it

If you put salt on a slug it dies. If you put sugar on it it dies.
Only the birds are God-made for sure. With insects it's hard to tell.

Every city-dweller is a chain-smoker. Every automobile
a license to kill. Car-carrying ocean vessels transport heavy cargo

over long distances by the thousands.
To curb a pest problem in your home, you might

want to put poison into the corners of your kitchen,
maybe next to food, some nothing

cabinet. You may get a rat or a mouse this way.
Its body slows down, its breathing, until it dies.

If you find one on the street that's been poisoned,
cover it. Find a lone gardening glove nearby, or child's sock. Don't

cover its eyes. It has to be able to see the cars and people passing
so it knows it won't be stepped on before it goes.

There are two ways I know of to load a car onto an ocean vessel.
The first is like a thousand rodents boarding the Ark. The other

is like a woman passing off an infant to a sister or cousin.
Clusters of cranes wait at ports off the coasts to do this.

**surge**


remember when Tuan
scored that goal against the neighbors
and then pumped his fist and
slid across the lawn,
how the grass stained
his knee-highs?

• • • • •

feline on the prowl. Nip's 5 a.m. shuffle.
rooster at sunrise, ears
cocked back, springing forward. and now
that two-pronged tear just inches
above the hem of your pant leg.

• • • • •

when coming home with mom and dad
from Sunday lunch at grandpa's—okra in spit soup
with rice—little brother napped, his cheek
pressed against my shoulder, drool
thickening the knit, darkening the faded green
of my right sleeve.

# wristwatch

*Đâu?* As in *where*. Where are my keys? My dad had a keychain with 30 keys, maybe more—how many he actually used, I'm not sure. Both my parents, like me, are the kind of disorganized people who know where everything is. T-o-u-r-b-i-l-l-o-n. The word that eliminated me from the 6th grade spelling bee. *Tourbillon:* May you please use it in a sentence? Jonathan Stroud afterwards mocked me for getting the word wrong: *How many l's does it have?* I wanted to smack him upside the head using the same keychain my father used on me. My uncle used cigarette tobacco to stop the bleeding. How could I make something like that up? Good Will Hunting, little Willie, from Southie with 12 older brothers. *Do you know all their names.* Of course, they're my brothers. *What are they called?* Marky Ricky Danny Terry Mikey Davy Timmy Tommy Joey Robbie Johnny and Brian. *Say it again.* Marky Ricky Danny Terry Mikey Davy Timmy Tommy Joey Robbie Johnny and Brian. Can you spell *Tourbillon.* Of course, I already got it wrong once.

## whispers

To hear me, you had to lean in closely.
Your room was cold at night, the window
propped open by a tall picture frame.

Our foreheads touching, I watched my breath
obscure your mouth. Your mouth, the only visible part
of your face—you rarely looked this good.

We sat listening to children playing in the yard
below your window, trying to single out your
little sister's laugh. You couldn't find it, in the dark.

## allegory for family members

Bà Ngoại, who will pray for me
when you are gone?

     the master of ceremonies with her microphone

     a young child making hand
     shadows over palm
     leaves during a sermon

     the braids of a toy mare

     the mare

Did my confession make us closer? I killed the pope. Huddled next to
you, burrowed along your side, face down in supplication: I'm ruined,
I've been corrupted forever, Bà Ngoại. When you told everyone I was
your favorite, was this before or after I confessed? One's the prodigal
son, the other is his brother. Either story works for me. On my
birthday, too many lines and the pope dies.

     guilt, Catholic gifts

     red and gold paper
     packets wasted on games

the green banana ripening

red dust lining the lip of the new year's vase

**expecting**


Every time the cat went missing, it went

missing for days. Nights, you

left the windows open. Some of the screens were

missing. House full of insects—I had to pull

june bugs from the couch cushions,

the bedsheets, your shirt once. Sometimes

they left their little legs behind. *Hard*

*little fishbone hooks at the back of my throat*

*when I was a boy. A priest brought communion*

*to my house. My tongue was the altar. The wafer*

*dissolved over it, and the sharp bone melted a little.*

*He wore a green scarf—two men were pulling gold*

*straight from a river, a halo like the sun, some eyes*

*like luck—and asked me which saints I prayed to.*

From the porch light, I saw your stomach

rise and fall. The curl of your upper lip

made you look resentful. The browning purple

your mouth took on in that light. We did laps

around the pond. Both of us spoke in loud voices.

## lake hoàn kiếm

The wind plays with the moon; the moon with the wind.
The moon sets. Who can the wind play with?

—Vietnamese folk song

Meet me on the unlit stretch of lake least fooled
by autumn. Under the youngest willow.

Its thin branches hang over me, its leaves
veil my face from the milk flower playing
matchmaker.

You say you love her sweet scent.
Even the plum blossom isn't so lavish.

One day I will take a wife myself.
If I reach forward, I can touch the water
past the edge of the moon.

I wait for you beyond the temple lights
at the center of the lake, my ankles deep
in a pillar of moon on the water.

Come whisper our secrets to the lake,
make it shiver in unison with the willow.
Shall we become now
worthy of the Lạc-Hồng race?

## prayer in writing

When I pray, I often pray to Bà Ngoại.
When I write, I always have in mind a living reader.
When I pray, I pray for myself.
When I write, it's the same.

I've prayed to Bà that she pray for me.
I've prayed to God to help me pray genuinely.

I write in symbol:
committing the unforgivable sin, I adulterate prayer with metaphor,
asking God to make me less like Jacob, and more like Esau.
But in praying this,
I become Jacob.

When I pray, I shouldn't use words.
When I write, I shouldn't use prayer.
I should write as I pray.
Or I should stop writing.

## history lesson from anh hai

I spoke to Great-Aunt tonight. She sounded like her sister.
It had been fifty years since they'd last spoken; mom said they cried
    over the phone.
Bà Nội used to always tell me, *Đi tu đi con*. But I know
The difference between *tu* and *tù* is one mark.

Fifty years since they'd last spoken; mom said they cried.
The night dad disappeared into a jungle, Bà Nội also cried.
The difference between *tu* and *tù* is one mark.
Once I heard about a monk who died setting himself on fire.

Bà Nội cried the night dad disappeared into a jungle.
It was a sad time. A nun and monk were made to fornicate in the
    street.
Once I heard about a monk who died setting himself on fire.
Twenty years later the rodent problem—200 đồng per severed tail.

It was a sad time. A nun and monk were made to fornicate in the
    street.
Bà Nội used to always say, *Đi tu đi con*. But I know.
Twenty years later the rodent problem—200 đồng per severed tail.
I spoke to Great-Aunt tonight. She sounded like Bà Ngoại.

## the mercedes out front


If one
is disciplined,

if one saves
faithfully,

one can buy
              things one likes:

like the neighbor's
Bichon
Frise

who is as we speak

taking a shit
in the alleyway by the dumpster;

a condom wrapper
bristles like a firecat
in the wind.

Or is it better to be off leash?

Everything here was once an evergreen.

*Mà*

## the cowboy

A cowboy tipped his hat at my mother, once. I'd never
seen that before. Something almost understanding
in his demeanor. Not at all the regard of others like him—
that steady gaze, less like watching a blue jay
or a cardinal, and more like watching a pigeon;
the quiet amusement which comes from wondering
how it is a bird can grow so plump.

Years later, after seeing her home village
for the first time since the war, my mother comes back
with fresh childhood details—tall ceramic vats
cooking fish sauce in the sun, dried squid laid out
on porches pummeled into shredding by pestles
like small baseball bats. The polite gestures—
the old women singing by the busy brook, the young
wives passing by them, bowing, carrying away
with them a song about a mother egret.

## hedgehog in the fog

*After Yuriy Norshteyn*

(hedgehog)

He imagines the horse is powerful: How is it that
she is there in the fog?

But, her head
is in the clouds,

she is only partially
in the fog.

(owl)

Wise, not clever—
never had an original idea; imitates the hedgehog
the hedgehog;

talks to his other self in the well.
The echoes surprise him,
they surprise his other self.

(bat)

The magical bat:
the closest thing we have
to the butterfly.

 (bear)

The bear is too much in the sun. He cannot count
the stars.

He is too slow to say much, too slow
to understand much,

yet talks a great deal, which both eases
and makes worse his anxiety.

 (horse)

Noble.

There's nothing as ethereal
as a spirit in a wood.

 (dog)

Finds things,
returns them to their owner.

Is helpful, is friendly, provides
assurance.

 (crocodile)

Is helpful.

(hedgehog)

The hedgehog can
count stars.

## chores for the oldest daughter

If the sky is cold, ladle out porridge
for your brother. In the evening, sing him

a song. He is my fish, you my cat.
Sing about the river sage. Bring home

chrysanthemum. Take two coins for the old
blind man. Remember to greet him for me.

If he has some wisdom, thank him. Do not dawdle.
Return home before the kettle whistles.

The chrysanthemum, leave the fresh buds
on the mantle for another time,

and give me what's left of the dried ones.
Watch them become the river's edge again.

**s u r g e**


The smooth crackling
twinkling above
*a lipstick's traces*

like soft snaps of a fire

reminds me there
is such a thing
as another time

another place

## rat-tat-tat

We heard *Changes* three times on the radio. First on the way to
Salem. Again on the way to the grocery store on the way back from
Salem. And then again on the way to pick up Becky and Dave. At
some point during all that, we also heard Biggie twice. It was you
that noticed this, not me—I couldn't recall the first time. All night
we drank a lot. And when Becky and Dave left, you loaded up shots
for me, you, my sister and her boyfriend. You drank more than
everybody. I had to give you big big waters between each shot. You
pounded them all down to prove a point. I was really surprised. At
the end of the night, I helped you get ready for bed. You were in the
bathroom, slouching, hunched over, standing in the middle of the
room. I was holding another big big water. You were crying into my
chest. I closed the door behind me and asked you what you needed
next. "I want Tupac to be alive again." You were sobbing louder than
ever. When you came to, you drank half a big big water, brushed your
teeth, but didn't wash your face.

## post-mortem with my little brother

Pre-

One thing that's
never happened:
working honestly
while not
thinking about
family.

•••••

The bullet
tears
but we don't say
it has hands.

One night I look up
and bang
our family
has torn our family
apart forever.

•••••

Post-

One thing that's
never happened:
working honestly
while not
thinking about
family.

## the roundworm travels up from the foot

*(Having to have a body)*

Survival instincts: I turn myself into a smaller target. Thriving
    instincts: I put myself into situations where my pupils dilate.

*(Boxing)*

To make yourself into a smaller target. You're a beautiful silhouette,
    revealing only one shoulder at a time, constantly rotating
    clockwise behind the heel of your pivot foot.
Avoid the left hook, the left shot to the body, the straight right. Keep
    your rhythm.

*(Dancing)*

In the dark, with the music, there's no need to be a silhouette; your
    shoulders can be square to others. One goal: to be a string
    undulating between two fixed points.
Move sharply and quickly if you're not feeling graceful tonight;
    slowly if you're feeling confident and have nothing to hide or if
    your pupils are especially alive.

*(Mermaid birth)*

The amniotic sac is intact and someone has to puncture it. Then
baby's song: so brave and so beautiful. His rotator cuff, the
　　examining table, unused forceps and ventouse.

Silver nitrate
eye drops: then Judy Garland is in color.


*(The roundworm travels up from the foot only to be swallowed again)*

I ran first thing in the morning, sub-24 minute 3-miles. I'm the
　　fastest. Today is a big day in a big way. Hot shower, a half-mile
　　walk to the T.
It has been at least 12 hours since I consumed salt. I am cold, fresh
　　water. I am the whale
bursting out of the Arctic.


*(Boxing)*

You're beautiful as a silhouette, in and out in and out. Masterful. You
　　made weight again;
hydrate back to 134. Don't let your shoulders be square to anyone.
　　Don't be the midpoint of the base of an isosceles.

*(Dancing)*

I ran first thing in the morning, sub-24 3-miles. I'm the fastest. Hot
　　shower, a half-mile walk to the T.

It has been at least 12 hours since I had salt. On the train, the guy
    sitting across from me has
what must be vomit on his shoes, not caked on but still glistening.
    Like me, he is purged.
He is cold, fresh water.


*(Buckeyes)*

We piled them up
for ammunition. We lay down with them
among the bruised leaves so that we could
rise, shining.


*(The roundworm travels up from the foot again)*

Shower, Clobetasol foam, Dove Men-Care Post-Shave Balm,
Tretinoin cream, Joico Matte Clay or Molding Clay or Water Resistant
    Styling Glue. An apple.


*(Boxing)*

Brody fails to make weight


*(Dancing)*

I'll move
slowly tonight. Madonna, Laurent
Korcia, Iron and Wine.

*(Buckeyes)*

We piled them up
for ammunition. We lay down with them
so that we could
rise, shining.


*(Dancing)*

Ecstasy turns us into moths.

I'm an embryo in the mother's womb.
I sleep hidden in you.
Don't give birth to me yet.


*(Dilated pupils)*

Hyperbole and the coquette.


*(Mermaid birth)*

The amniotic sac is intact and someone has to puncture it. Then
mother's wooing: so overwhelming, so alluring. New Order,
Erasure, Lorde, glitter, eyeliner. Judy Garland is in color.

## another way of explaining it

A fine way of looking at things—
me observing you kissing me.

How decent of me
to pretend I am shocked by you.

You're the inverted foot that starts a line:
that start of a climb that
begins with falling.

## scuttle

Rats can scuttle; they can also
bound. But unlike squirrels,
who also bound, rats scatter
much faster when a human
suddenly interjects itself
and makes a scene, revealing fruit
sprinkled naked at the curb.
Squirrels, when they scatter
and reach a safe distance,
slow their bound, like a train
fading into a station, welcomed by
a scuttle on the drum—stage
introduction for the rodent's
scuttle across the lawn
before bounding, becoming
flexibly upright and entering
flight and landing for its
climb up the skinny trunk
of a crabapple tree.

## tội nghiệp, cat

With your one eye, your only eye, at a safe distance, you bat
at your sister, making contact just
above her eyeliner.

.....

The week of the Champions League Final, three times you
snuck past me through the

front door. I took it to mean Messi
would steal behind United's back four

and score.

.....

Every morning around five:
a few pill bottles, the Ott-Lite, a coffee
mug. Crepuscular

motherfucker. I wonder if you'll ever
let me get to six a.m.

.....

In Vietnam I think they would've called
you little tiger. I think you would've made
some farmer a little money.

Severed rat tails by the bunch saving rice crops.

. . . . .

With a gob of turkey fat in your mouth
you leap down off
the counter.

Mighty hunter. The other cats never
take their eyes off you.

## rickshaw boy

The man I pulled tonight
carried a load of books.

When I felt him watching
me uphill, I grimaced.

He gave me lunar
cakes the size

of two camel humps.
When I answered him,

I smiled to his face.
He wore the moonlight

in his specs. Pant
seams clean as the embroidery

work of his book covers.
One cannot grow rich

without a bit of cleverness.
Should I have shown

him the secret of my deft
touch? The Circling Moon,

the Graceful Swan? How East
Wind beats West Wind

if other two winds say so?
Snow falls on cedars.

## study habits

In our first living room my parents had
a painting of a deserted beach.

One day I send a toy knife flipping towards it.
I let it go too soon. From between my thumb and forefinger,

the point. Fifty-fifty chance the handle rescues.
Instead, the blade finds its stopping point

somewhere in the blue sky or white cloud
of a happy beach—calm waves, wooden posts
beginning their lean parallel to the ocean line.

Tall weeds sprout out of sand mounds, like hairs
growing out of the mole on my uncle's face.

The rip in the canvas is a locale for sprouting, too—
some seagulls overhead, some far away

over the ocean. The ocean, the way I learned
to draw birds: lazy checkmarks depicting flight in the distance.

## soccer

> Nothing is so beautiful as Messi in the Spring.
>
> (Traditional)

*Lady with an Ermine,* the Leonardo
found with a boot mark in the cellar
of a Polish noble's country estate.

Apparently there was supposed to be a Raphael
alongside it. It's the hope of scholars that the missing
painting will resurface one day, maybe
having survived the underworld
where it was used as currency.

Imagine Zidane in the basement of the Louvre,
his goal in the European Final
at Hampden Park. Or Messi's header
against United in Rome when he lost his right shoe.

Leonardo rhymes with
the Tapestry of the Apostolic Palace. Messi does not rhyme with
the fire outside the opera house in Berlin.

## notes

*Epigraph*

From "The Dance," from *The Complete Poems of Hart Crane,* edited by Marc Simon. Copyright 1933, 1958, 1966 by Liveright Publishing Corporation. Copyright © 1986 by Marc Simon. Used by permission of Liveright Publishing Corporation.

*Section Titles*

*Ca*—Sing
*Tìm*—Seek
*Mà*—But, Although

*We Play a Game Using Tomatoes*

*cà*—tomato
*ca*—sing
*chua*—sour
*cá*—fish
*chùa*—temple
*cà chua*—tomato

*Romanticizing Vietnam*

The phrase "shook grief's rattle" is adapted from John Balaban's translation of a Hồ Xuân Hương poem, which is titled "Confession I," in Balaban's collection of translations: *Spring Essence: The Poetry of Hồ Xuân Hương* (Copper Canyon Press, 2000). Used by permission of the translator.

*Love Trinkets*

Indebted to Marie Howe's poem "On Men, Their Bodies," from *Magdalene* (W.W. Norton, 2017).

Inspired by pieces from the Chinese, Japanese, Korean, and Asian Export Art collections at the Peabody Essex Museum; eighteen pieces, mostly from the 18th and 19th centuries, including kimonos, fans, combs, and one fish-shaped snuff bottle.

"One lover was bold and touched/me once behind a door, but it was her cousin/Vandie, the one who never looked at me, that I loved": adapted from Edith Wharton's 1920 novel *The Age of Innocence*.

"The earth shook, a portal opened, we stepped through it": adapted from Danielle Legros Georges's poem "Intersection," from *The Dear Remote Nearness of You* (Barrow Street Press, 2016). Permission to quote lines from "Intersection," with changed text and lineation, was granted by the author.

"*having to have a body*": from Frank Bidart's poem "Writing Ellen West," from *Metaphysical Dog* (Farrar, Straus and Giroux, 2013). Used by permission of Farrar, Straus and Giroux.

"We learned to catch the trout's moon whisper": adapted from "The Dance," from *The Complete Poems of Hart Crane*, edited by Marc Simon. Copyright 1933, 1958, 1966 by Liveright Publishing Corporation. Copyright © 1986 by Marc Simon. Permission to quote lines from "The Dance," with changed text and lineation, was granted by Liveright Publishing Corporation.

"*Lovely, little,* lastly, *likely*": inspired by lines from Robert Pinsky's poem "The Want Bone," from *The Want Bone* (Ecco Press, 1990): "But O I love you it sings, my little . . . my flower my fin my life my lightness my O." Reprinted with the permission of the author.

*Dancing School*
Incidents from the 2011 Champions League Final, between FC Barcelona and Manchester United, at Wembley Stadium in London. Xavi Hernández, Carles Puyol, Andrés Iniesta, and Lionel Messi—all players for Barcelona, who won the match 3–1.

The epigraph is taken from Elizabeth Bishop's poem "A Cold Spring," from *Elizabeth Bishop: The Complete Poems 1927–1979* (Farrar, Straus and Giroux, 2013) and *Poems* (Chatto & Windus, 2011). Used by permission of Farrar, Straus and Giroux; and The Random House Group Limited.

*Duet*

"The Right Time" is a 1957 song recorded by Nappy Brown. In 1958 Ray Charles released his own version of the song with Margie Hendricks and the Raelettes singing backup. In 1959 Charles's version reached number five in the Billboard R&B chart. The song is especially memorable for Hendricks's virtuosic solo. Used by permission of Sony/ATV Music Publishing and Hal Leonard Permissions.

*First-Person Plural*

*Em*—little brother or little sister
*Chị*—older sister
*Thím*—auntie (wife of paternal uncle)
*Chú*—uncle
*Mấy em*—little cousins
*Mẹ*—mother
*Bố*—father
*Ông Nội*—paternal grandfather
*Bác*—uncle or auntie (older than our parents)
*Cô*—auntie (younger sister of our father)
*Út*—youngest in the family

52 Pickup: "Any deck of cards will do. 'Unnecessary' cards such as jokers may be ceremoniously removed. The game mechanics require at least one player who is familiar with the game and one player who wants to be initiated into the game. The first player, as 'dealer,' throws the entire deck into the air so the cards land strewn on the floor. The other player must then pick them up" (https://en.wikipedia.org/wiki/52_Pickup).

*Ask Mr. Owl*

The phrase "How many licks does it take to get to the Tootsie Roll center of a Tootsie Pop?" was first introduced in an animated commercial on U.S. television in 1969. In the commercial, a boy poses the question to a cow, a fox, a turtle and then finally an owl (https://en.wikipedia.org/wiki/Tootsie_Pop).

In the Gospel according to Matthew, the disciple Peter asks Jesus, "Lord, how many times could my brother sin against me and I forgive him? As many as seven times?" To which Jesus replies, "I tell you, not as many as seven; but seventy times seven."

*Three Tongue Twisters*

The epigraph is a childhood tongue twister. The other three twisters are originals.

*Allegory for Family Members*

*Bà Ngoại*—maternal grandmother

*Lake Hoàn Kiếm*

The epigraph is a translation of the Vietnamese *ca dao* (folk poetry/song) entitled "Linked Verses," in John Balaban's collection of translations, *Ca Dao Vietnam* (Copper Canyon Press, 2003). Used by permission of the translator.

*Prayer in Writing*

*Bà Ngoại*—maternal grandmother

*History Lesson from Anh Hai*

*Anh Hai*—older brother, the oldest son
*Bà Nội*—paternal grandmother
*Đi tu đi con*—enter the priesthood, my child
*tu*—novitiate, seminary or convent
*tù*—prison
*Bà Ngoại*—maternal grandmother

*The Mercedes Out Front*

"bristles like a firecat": adapted from Wallace Stevens's poem "Earthy Anecdote," from *Harmonium*.

"Everything here was once an evergreen": inspired by the last line of Rita Dove's poem "Old Folks Home, Jerusalem," from *Grace Notes* (W.W. Norton, 1989).

*Hedgehog in the Fog*
    *Hedgehog in the Fog* is a 1975 animated film directed by Soviet/ Russian filmmaker Yuriy Norshteyn.

*Surge*
    "*a lipstick's traces*": from Eric Maschwitz and Jack Strachey's song "These Foolish Things," rendition by Billie Holiday.

*The Roundworm Travels up from the Foot*
    "*Having to have a body*": Frank Bidart (see above note on "Love Trinkets")

    "We piled them up/for ammunition. We lay down with them/ among the bruised leaves so that we could/rise, shining": adapted from Rita Dove's poem "The Buckeye," from *Grace Notes* (W.W. Norton, 1989). Permission to quote lines from "The Buckeye," with changed lineation, was granted by the author.

    "I'm an embryo in the mother's womb./I sleep hidden in you./ Don't give birth to me yet.": adapted from Anna Swir's poem "The Iron Hedgehog," from *Happy as a Dog's Tail* (Harcourt Brace Jovanovich, 1985), translation by Czesław Miłosz with Leonard Nathan. Used by permission of Mr. Czesław Miłosz and the Estate of Anna Swir, c/o Sterling Lord Literistic, Inc.

*Tội Nghiệp, cat*
    In the 2009 Champions League Final, Lionel Messi scored FC Barcelona's second goal to effectively seal the victory against Manchester United at the Stadio Olimpico in Rome. Barcelona won the match 2–0.

*Soccer*
    "Nothing is so beautiful as Spring": from Gerard Manley Hopkins' poem "Spring" (Elizabeth Bishop uses this Hopkins line as the epigraph of her poem "A Cold Spring").

In the 2009 Champions League Final, FC Barcelona's Argentinian, Lionel Messi, scored with a header, for him an atypical goal. In the melee of the goal, Messi's right shoe came off, and he had to retrieve it before celebrating, which involved kissing the shoe. One slow-motion close-up of the match reveals a small logo of the Argentina flag on his footwear.

In the 2001 Champions League Final, Real Madrid's French soccer great, Zinedine Zidane, scored a stunning goal to win the match, considered by some to be the greatest goal ever scored in a final.

# acknowledgments

Grateful acknowledgment to the following publications in which these poems first appeared, sometimes in slightly different versions:

*The Adroit Journal*: "The Roundworm Travels Up from the Foot" and "We Play a Game Using Tomatoes"

*Amethyst Arsenic*: "Engagement Ring" and "You"

*COG*: "Dancing School" and "Surge"

*Connotation Press: An Online Artifact*: "Expecting"

*The Cortland Review*: "Soccer"

*The Journal*: "Hedgehog in the Fog"

*Poetry Magazine*: "Mother's Dirge" and "Rickshaw Boy"

*Poetry Northwest*: "Bridge Ghosts," "First-Person Plural," and "Tội Nghiệp, cat"

*Slate*: "History Lesson from Anh Hai"

*TAYO*: "Allegory for Family Members" and "Prayer in Writing"

*TRACK//FOUR*: "Chores for the Oldest Daughter," "Romanticizing Vietnam," "Spelling Out My Name, or Proof of the Military Industrial Complex," and "Spelling Out My Name in Vietnamese, or Proof of the Military Industrial Complex"

*TriQuarterly*: "The Cowboy" and "Poem with a Rat in It"

Special thanks to Massachusetts Cultural Council and St. Botolph Club for their support.

Deep gratitude to Carl Phillips, whose generosity, advice, and skill helped bring this book into its final form.

To my teachers, whose kindness and mentorship got me through school—Oscar Casares, Louise Glück, Jackie Greenfield, Ha Jin, Judith Kroll, Robert Levine, Thomas Pruitt, Betty Sitton, Joseph Slate, Rosanna Warren, and David Wevill; especially to Martin Kevorkian, who gave me all of the most important tools, and to Robert Pinsky, without whose guidance and musical gifts I would not have this book.

To my grandparents, for their love and wisdom—Ông Bà Ngoại and Ông Bà Nội.

To my friends and loved ones, for their talents and massive hearts—Larry Alam, Cesar Benítez, Marlon Braddock, Trisha Chakrabarti, Kevin Crotty, Toan Đô, Uyên Đô, Bishop Goguen, James Harper, Brian Heine, Kalyn Horst, Lisa Landry, Lorna Landry, Dan Lien, Bob-O March, Grace Muron, Lý Hữu Nguyễn, Brady Patterson, Kay Fox Petrucci, Ryn Arrants Petrucci, Ellen Pinsky, Becky Simpkins, Jess X Snow, Tomasz Wawyrzniak, Winarto Wongso, and Amanda Zhang.

To my poet friends and loved ones, for their enthusiasm, brilliance, and ever-seeking souls—Tamiko Beyer, Wo Chan, Misha Chowdhury, Catherine Con, East Meets West Bookstore, Ying-Ju Lai, Paul Trần, Tsen Ga Tsung, and Tomas Unger; especially to my first and second readers—Judson Evans, Laura Marris, Christine Mastrangelo, and Sara Rivera, whose encouragement and insights helped make my manuscript possible.

To my Kundiman family, especially Cathy Linh Chế, Oliver de la Paz, Sarah Gambito, and Joseph O. Legaspi, for making chosen family real.

To my most intimate support group—Bridge, Emily, Mây Hôa, and Nghiệp, for being there always.

And finally, to my two biggest inspirations—my partner Allison Landry and my brother Tuấn Đoàn. I will never be able to repay you for what you've given me.